Dedication...

This book is dedicated to my son, TJ. Never compare yourself to anyone else. If you compare yourself to someone you think is doing better than you, you may lose motivation to continue growing. If you compare yourself to someone you believe you are doing better than, you may stop developing because you think you've already maxed out your growth. Always compare yourself to the best version of you that you can be. This will inspire you to continue striving to reach your full potential.

You are going to accomplish great things. I'm already so proud of you!

~Mommy

This book belongs to...

TJ is awesome! He learned to
crawl and then to walk.
He even learned to run.
Now, he is learning his name and
how to talk.

TJ loves his stuffed elephant, Mr. Bubbles! He hugs him tight when he watches cartoons.
When it's time to eat, TJ even feeds him with a spoon.

TJ also has a teddy bear, Mr. Fuzzy Wuzzy. And as he falls asleep at night... He cuddles with the bear while he holds Mr. Bubbles tight.

One night, TJ had a dream he was at the pet store because he loves dogs. He especially loves the sounds they make...WOOF WOOF WOOF! TJ and his friends pointed to the dogs and laughed with excitement. All of the dogs were saying WOOF WOOF WOOF!

TJ enjoys watching trains as they go by. He even likes to listen to their sound...CHOO CHOO!
TJ is so awesome that his parents bought him a toy train with train tracks that were round. CHOO CHOO!

TJ is very smart! He can match letters and numbers. He even put his toy train set together by himself. His mommy and daddy were surprised that he didn't need any help.

However, TJ does need help with responding to his name and learning how to say words. His mommy and daddy are helping him. And he is working hard every day to learn.

Hi.
My name is TJ..

After all, he is a champ! And there is nothing that TJ can't do. TJ's daddy called his name while they were at the park and he turned his head to respond. Whoo Hoo!

At daycare, he is even learning how to use sign language. Sign language will help others know when he is hungry or thirsty. TJ is awesome because he is learning quickly.

TJ never feels bad because other kids can say more words. "You are our smart little man," TJ's parents always tell him. "Everyone has a different way they learn."

TJ is grateful because he knows that everyone is different. And that everyone does things at their own pace.
His mommy always tells him that learning is not a race.

TJ's mommy gave him Mr. Bubbles and told him that a dog can have multiple puppies in a couple months while it takes an elephant two years to have one baby. And it doesn't matter who has theirs the fastest because all the babies are loved greatly.

TJ's mommy looked at him and said, "I love you just the same." Then she said, "Can you tell mommy your name?"

TJ stood up quickly and smiled as if he had something to say. He looked at his mom and said,
"Hi, my name is TJ."
TJ's mommy jumped for joy and his daddy did too. They were so proud of TJ because there is nothing he can't do.
TJ is awesome! He learned to crawl and then to walk. He even learned to run. And now he has learned his name and how to talk.